The Trial of

John Kimber

For the Murder of Two Female Negro Slaves, on Board the Recovery, African Slave Ship Tried at the Admiralty Sessions, Held at the Old Baily, the 7th of June, 1792

Student of the Temple

Alpha Editions

This edition published in 2024

ISBN : 9789362096760

Design and Setting By
Alpha Editions
www.alphaedis.com
Email - info@alphaedis.com

Contents

INTRODUCTION. ....- 1 -

THE TRIAL OF CAPTAIN JOHN KIMBER,
For Murder, &c. ....- 2 -

INTRODUCTION.

ON a business which has so long agitated the public mind as the Slave Trade, every thing that can be said, must in some manner be interesting. The atrocity of that unnatural and abominable custom could not in any instance have been more abundantly manifested, than in the late decision of a large majority in the House of Commons.

Perhaps the procrastination of the same important question, in a superior House, may be productive of greater good than the people of England are aware of. Perhaps it may upon the next discussion lead to an immediate and total abolition of a cruel and inhumanvi traffic. It cannot but be lamented that a personage of the first rank, who could have no other motive except that of love for uncontroulable tyranny, should become so strenuous an advocate for slavery. He has more than once expressed his sentiments in public, and on the present occasion seemed to have comported himself with an extraordinary degree of zeal, which whether it became the dignity of a P——— in such a cause, we shall not take on us to determine, but leave it to the world to judge of the propriety of such conduct.

Whatever the public opinion may be relative to the prosecution carried on against Captain Kimber, who has been (we suppose fairly) acquitted by an English Jury, it was evidently a necessary and a useful measure. It may afford a salutary lesson to those captains of slave ships, and masters of slaves who should hereafter attempt to commit such horrid outrages as he has been charged with: and it may, from the circumstances here related, (for such barbarities have doubtless been often practised) fill the minds of men universally with horror against the present system: until tyranny shall at length give way to public opinion, and liberty and happiness be restored to human beings.

THE TRIAL OF CAPTAIN JOHN KIMBER,

For Murder, &c.

THIS trial came on at the Admiralty Sessions held at the Old Baily, on Thursday the 7th of June 1792; before Sir James Marriot, Judge Advocate of the Admiralty, Mr. Justice Ashurst, and Mr. Baron Hotham.

The prisoner was indicted for having feloniously, wickedly, and with malice aforethought, beaten and tortured a female slave, so as to cause her death: and he was again indicted for having caused the death of another female slave.

Mr. Broderic on the side of the prosecution, first opened the cause.

Sir William Scott next stated, that the prisoner, Captain Kimber, had commanded the ship RECOVERY, which traded in slaves from the Coast of Africa, to the West Indies: that in 1791, he arrived in the river of Calabar, whence he had, in some time after, departed with a cargo of slaves, among whom was that negro girl, for whose murder the prisoner now stood indicted. She had been for a considerable time afflicted with a loathsome distemper, and a lethargic complaint, which prevented her from eating, or mixing in any of those exercises which the other slaves on board were accustomed to practice. The prisoner had her punished for this supposed obstinacy; flogged her, and had her raised up by pullies from the deck, so that the tortures she endured, caused her to languish for a few days, until she died.

I shall not, said the learned Council, enter into a detail of circumstances, for that must appear by the evidence which is to be laid before you Gentlemen of the Jury. Nor is it necessary that I should make any observations on the heinousness of this offence, as that is the province of the Court. And no doubt, your verdict will be given with that discretion and impartiality, which has always been shewn on similar occasions.

Mr. Thomas Dowling was first called, and examined by Mr. Attorney General; he had been a surgeon on board the RECOVERY, the ship which the prisoner commanded: in the beginning of June, he had arrived in the river of Calabar, on the coast of Africa, where in the end of August they had compleated their cargo of slaves. About the time of sailing, he had under his care, a female slave, aged about fourteen or fifteen years, who had been afflicted with a virulent gonorrhea, and lethargy, or drowsy complaint, of which latter ailment he could never learn the real cause. She was not then in a convalescent state: but her diseases were stationary, and bore every probable appearance of recovery. In this situation she could not eat, as the other slaves did, nor join in any of their amusements, at which the Captain was so irritated, that he used to flog her himself, with a whip, the handle of which, was one foot long, and the lash two. About three weeks after they had sailed, he beat her in this manner with uncommon severity; and on the 22d of December, perceiving her not to dance with the other negro women, he ordered a boy to bring a teakle, one end of which was fastened to the *mizen stay* and the other to one of her hands, and by this she was lifted up from the deck, and remained suspended for about five minutes: and during that time, she was bounsed up and down, or in other words, lifted up, and let fall again, by the way, who had a hold of the teakle.

She was then taken down and suspended in the same manner by the other arm. She was next lifted up by one leg; and afterwards by the other: until at last she was taken up for the fifth time by both hands, and underwent the fifth excruciating suspension. The whole time from the first to the last suspension, this witness said might have been half an hour.

While she continued hung up by both hands, the prisoner lashed her inhumanly with his whip: and when she was let down, he forced her to walk without any assistance down the hatchway: this she was unable to do, having got but two or three steps, when she slipt all the rest of the way.

When this witness next saw her she was welted in several parts of the body, her hands were swelled in consequence of the hanging, and her legs disfigured in a shocking manner: after this the witness saw her in convulsions, had her brought on deck, and rubbed her with volatile spirits; but every remedy was ineffectual: she languished away in this miserable state for three days, and on the third expired.

All this happened in the middle passage about 200 leagues from Granada, whither the RECOVERY with her cargo was bound. And the witness was positive that the death of the slave was occasioned by the ill treatment she had received.

The witness was cross-examined by Mr. Pigott leading council for the prisoner.

Q. Has it been your undeviating opinion that the girl died in consequence of the punishment said to have been inflicted on her?

A. It has.

Q. Was her death the subject of no conversation at that time among the ship's crew?

A. It was between me and Mr. Devereux; and I heard the two boys Pearson and Cruise speak of it.

Q. How many men did the whole crew consist of?

A. About six and twenty.

Q. At what time of the day did the fact happen which you have related?

A. Some time in the forenoon.

Q. You heard no conversation about it, except that between the two boys?

A. No.

Q. Are these boys now absent?

A. I heard so, but cannot say.

Q. How many of the mariners do you think are now in this country?

A. I do not know. I mean to relate every fact which may go, as well to subvert my own evidence, as make against the prisoner.

Q. What time did you arrive at Granada?

A. On the 28th of October.

Q. Did you disclose the death of this girl to any person at Granada?

A. No.

Q. How long were you there?

A. About a month.

Q. Did you go to the Custom-house while you were there?

A. I did.

Q. Did you keep a journal while you were on the middle passage?

A. Yes: of whites, but not of blacks.

Q. Did you deliver in your journal?

A. Yes.

Q. And swore to it?

A. The form of an oath was read to me, by a person sitting at a desk: I took the book, and returned it without swearing.

Q. Did you sign the journal as sworn to it?

A. Yes I did.

Here Mr. Pigott read his oath, which declared that his journal was a just and true one; and the attested copy being handed to the witness, he declared, he did not recollect whether he had signed it or not.

Q. Is not that your name to the oath—and is it false or true?

A. I do not recollect that I signed it.

Q. Is your bond discharged?

A. Yes, I produced this copy at Bristol, to have it discharged.

Q. Why did not the cause of the death of the negro girl appear in your journal?

A. The apprehensions I had for my own safety, while I sailed with the prisoner, prevented me from relating it.

Q. Is it from disclosing a barbarous murder?

A. Yes; because the prisoner and I had often quarrelled, and I might have been judged an improper evidence against him.

Q. At what place did you quarrel?

A. At the river of Calabar.

Q. Did you not mutiny?

A. Never.

Q. Did you not strike the prisoner?

A. I did, after he had abused and struck me on board his ship.

Q. You collared and held him?

A. Yes, at the cabin door; when the first and second mate came and seized me, and by the prisoner's orders, I was put into irons, where I continued twenty-four hours; and I was afterwards excluded from the cabin, and obliged to mess with the common men.

Q. Did you not tell a Mr. Jacks that you would be revenged on Captain Kimber?

A. No, I never said so.

Q. Did you not say you would work his ruin?

A. Never, there is not such baseness in my nature. I never made a declaration of the kind to any person: but I said I would advertise him for his treatment of me. After my arrival in Bristol about Christmas last, I applied to Mr. Jacks, who was part owner of the RECOVERY, for my wages: he only paid me a part of them: I then complained to him of Captain Kimber's treatment, but did not disclose the murder.

Q. Did you not tell a Mr. Riddle that you would ruin Captain Kimber?

A. No: but I said I would commence a suit against him for his severe treatment of me, and that I would put myself under the protection of the first king's ship I met with. This conversation took place before we sailed from Calabar.

Q. Did you never say any thing to the prisoner's servant?

A. No.

Q. Did you ever administer any mercury to the girl who died?

A. No: it was improper for her complaint.

Q. Can you pretend to say that the suspension of this girl, was intended as a punishment?

A. I shall not say that; but it was obvious that it was a punishment.

Q. Might not the Captain have had reason to conclude that this suspension was necessary?

A. He might have had a motive, but I did not know it: he never consulted any person in what he used to do; and he has often interrupted me in the discharge of my duty.

Q. In what part of the ship did the suspension take place?

A. On the awning deck.

Q. And when it happened in so open and conspicuous a situation, as that it was impossible it must not have been seen by the ship's company; why was it not a more general subject of conversation?

A. I suppose it was, but I had not an opportunity of hearing it, except between Pearson and Cruise.

Q. What was the cause of your having at length disclosed this murder with which you now charge the prisoner?

A. I was solicited by Mr. Lloyd, a Banker at Birmingham, to give an account of the firing on the Town of Calabar; and from that relation, this account followed as a casual circumstance. I told it to Mr. Wilberforce the day before he made his speech in the House of Commons: but I never intended to prosecute or appear in evidence against Captain Kimber.

Q. So then this murder remained a secret until the day before Mr. Wilberforce made his Speech in the House of Commons?

A. No: I told it to persons in private.

Q. How often had you sailed as a surgeon before this time?

A. That was my first voyage, and it shall be my last.

The witness was re-examined by Mr. Attorney General, in order to account for some of those circumstances which came out on his cross examination, and might go to invalidate his testimony.

He said that he and the two boys were on the awning deck when the girl was suspended; that between this deck and the other part of the ship there was a barricade about nine feet high, which prevented those persons in the fore-part from seeing what was done abaft. By this means many of the ship's crew, who were on deck, might have remained without seeing or knowing what was done to the girl. And this might have been the cause why the circumstance had not been generally spoken of on board. When I gave in my journal, said the witness, at Grenada, I wished to omit every mention of the Negro Girl, from the apprehensions I was under for my safety, not knowing what the prisoner might have done; I therefore wished to evade the oath which is made on those occasions, and accordingly when the officer tendered it to me I took the book from him, and returned it without kissing it: he was sitting at a desk and did not see me.

The witness requested that the Court would examine the log book, where they should see that this death, which he omitted in his journal, did really happen. And the prisoner he said had told him that a journal was a mere matter of form.

He said also that when Mr. Lloyd and Mr. Wilberforce had examined him relative to the firing upon the Town of Calabar, the latter gentleman questioned him as to the treatment of the slaves on board the ships, and it was upon that occasion he told him the circumstance of the murder for which the prisoner was now indicted; without having had the remotest intention of prosecuting him. And he moreover observed that outrages of that nature were so common on board the slave ships, that they were looked upon with as much indifference as any trifling occurrence; their frequency had rendered them familiar.

Stephen Devereux, the next witness on the side of the prosecution, was examined by Mr. Solicitor General.

He deposed, that he had sailed to the coast of Guinea in the *Wasp*, from whence after he arrived there, he changed as third mate into the RECOVERY, which sailed from Africa on the first of September; he remembered the deceased Negro Girl very well: after he had been ten days on board, he saw Captain Kimber endeavouring to straiten her knees which were bent and contracted, and afterwards flogging her with a whip. While I was standing said the witness, on the starboard side of the quarter deck, I saw the girl running up by the gun takle, which was fastened by a block to the mizen stay: she was suspended by one of her arms, and continued raised above the deck for four or five minutes; she was let down, and lifted up again by the other arm, and Pearson the boy who held the takle jerked the fall: In this situation the boys were endeavouring to make her legs strait. She was taken up the third time by one leg, and the fourth time by the other; after which she was suffered to remain on the deck for some time. In this situation with her head drooping between her knees, Captain Kimber, who was present during the whole of her torture, lifted her up, gave her a slap on the face, and said *the bitch is sulky*: and then again endeavoured to straiten the contraction in the knees, with the intention of inflicting punishment on her. The fifth and last time she was lifted up by both hands, but her feet touched the deck; and in this posture the prisoner flogged her severely. When she was about going down the hatchway he would not suffer any body to assist her, but said *the bitch is sulky she must find her own way*. After she had got down two or three steps with great struggling and difficulty, she slipt along the rest of the ladder. All this happened in the morning.

I saw her the next day, and helped her up on deck: she was in a very filthy and shocking condition, quite weak and feeble, her body was covered with whales and bruises; she was not put down along with the other women; but was suffered to languish until she died, on the third day after the suspension.

Q. What other persons belonging to the ship's company were in sight of this business, besides the Captain, the Surgeon, and yourself?

A. The man at the wheel, and one or two more.

He was cross-examined by Mr. Sylvester.

Q. Was you not dancing with the women, at the time this business was going forward?

A. I was looking at the women dancing; but when the girl was suffering the punishment, they attended more to it, than to any thing else.

Q. Were there any, and what other persons with you at the time?

A. I don't know.

Q. Could you attempt to say, that it was by way of punishment that the prisoner endeavoured to straiten the girl's knees?

A. I know of no other motive he could have.

Q. Why did you not mention this business at Grenada, on your arrival there?

A. I did not wish to concern myself about it, particularly as Captain Kimber had behaved to me as a friend. Besides, every seaman on board must have heard of, or known it: and the Surgeon and I have often talked of it since.

Q. Did you ever give any information of this affair, till you were sent for to London?

A. No.

Q. And when you appeared before the Magistrate in London, did you not say that you were ignorant of the cause of the girl's death?

A. I did, for the reason I already mentioned, being delicate of doing any thing that might endanger the prisoner's life. But I am now certain, that if she had not been punished in the manner she was, she would have lived, and been fit for market.

[Here Mr. Sylvester read the deposition of this witness, which was taken before Sir Sampson Wright, at Bow-street, about two months ago, when the prisoner at the Bar was brought before him, charged with the murder for which he was now tried: in this deposition the present witness Devereux had stated, that he did not believe the girl died in consequence of the punishment inflicted on her: a contrary testimony to which he now gave to the Court.]

Q. Did you venture to take any of your ship's crew along with you, to give evidence of this business you now swear to?

A. No, they were all taken up at Bristol, and sent away.

Q. Are there not some of them now in London?

A. I do not know.

Q. Were you not dismissed your ship as first mate for mutiny, while on the Coast of Africa?

A. No: I did not mutiny.

Q. Were you not charged with having mutinied, and tried before six Captains?

A. The charge against me was, giving the lie to the Captain.

(Here Mr. Sylvester read the charges against him wherein he was stated to be a pernicious, dangerous, and troublesome fellow, and accordingly was turned away from the Ship: but there was no specific offence mentioned.)

On his re-examination by Mr. Solicitor General, he said that he had mentioned the Murder of the slave to several persons, before he came to give evidence of the firing upon the town of Calabar: and to a Gentleman at Bristol, after Kimber had been brought up to town. He did not know where the rest of the Crew had been.

Captain Kimber he said was one of those who formed the Court, that tried him on the Coast of Africa; and that he afterwards took him into his ship and treated him in a friendly manner.

These two were the only witnesses who appeared on the side of the prosecution.

Mr. Walter Jacks was first called on behalf of the prisoner, and examined by Mr. Pigott.

He said he was a merchant in Bristol, and had a share in the RECOVERY, which the prisoner commanded. He knew the prisoner six years, for three or four of which he had been in his Service: and he was always satisfied with his conduct: for he was good to the ship's company. Mr. Dowling, who had been Surgeon to the ship attended this witness at Bristol to demand the balance of his wages, which had been due to him.

At that time he complained that Captain Kimber had engaged to allow him two privileged Slaves, and that afterwards he would give him but one. The witness told him it was impossible he could have double privilege, as one Slave was all that was ever given to the surgeon of that ship: but in paying him his wages, he gave him sterling money instead of currency; as a small compensation for the hardships he said he sustained.

On the tenth of last January, after Dowling had received his wages, and thanked the witness; he told him that Captain Kimber was a rascal and a cheat, and that he would ruin him if it was in his power. And immediately after the prisoner had been taken into custody, these words occurred to the witness.

Thomas Lawer lived at Birmingham, he had frequent conversations with Dowling about the slave trade, who said, he had frequent quarrels with Captain Kimber, in one of which he struck him, and was afterwards put in irons, turned out of the cabin, and obliged to eat salt provisions with the fore-mast men.

The Captain allowed him but one privileged slave, and had behaved very ill towards him, for which he was determined to be revenged. These words he often used.

Benjamin Riddle was examined by Mr. Morgan.

He said he had been Surgeon on board the *Thomas*, which was on the coast of Africa, at the same time with the RECOVERY. There he heard Dowling say, that he had been maltreated by Captain Kimber, and that he would ruin him if possible: that he had a memorandum in his possession, which he could produce against him, when he came home. The witness asked to see the paper, but Dowling would not shew it. This was a sober deliberate conversation, and Dowling thought he was speaking to a friend.

After this, the witness heard Captain Kimber say, that Dowling's conduct was so bad, he could not keep him: he used to bleed, when it was evidently dangerous, and commit other improprieties in his professional line.

The witness also knew Devereux to have been dismissed from the *Wasp* for mutiny.

Mr. Dowling was again called, and asked whether it was true, that he had told Mr. Jacks, Lawer, and Riddle, that he would be revenged of, and ruin Captain Kimber if he could. He persisted in his former assertion, and declared that he had never said any such thing. He told the Court, that if they would indulge him with a hearing, he should clear every matter to their satisfaction; but having proceeded in a desultory manner, he was prevented from speaking.

Captain Thomas Philips was examined by Mr. Knowles.

He deposed, that he was on the Coast of Africa when the prisoner was there. Devereux had been turned out of the *Wasp* for mutiny, and had acknowledged the charges against him to be true: and the witness knew him to be a bad man.

There were, he said, on board Captain Kimber's ship, great quantities of oranges, which Dowling used to give to the slaves. The witness told him often, that fruits were bad for them; that they would cause the flux, which disease, it appeared, the deceased girl was afflicted with: and he knew, for twenty years he had been in that climate, such diseases carry off persons in the space of two days.

The witness knew the prisoner since he was at school, and he never heard any thing injurious to his character, until the present charge was preferred against him. He was always humane and good natured.

Thomas Lancaster was a mate belonging to the *Wasp*. He said, that Devereux had admitted the charges made against him: and all the ship's company looked on him as a dangerous fellow. After he had been turned out of the ship, he remained on shore for two months; and if Captain Kimber had not taken him under his protection, it would be impossible to tell what should become of him.

Devereux was again called, and questioned, as to the truth of what had been said against him: and he declared it was as false as that *one* was *two*.

He was proceeding to make a defence, when the Jury said they were all satisfied from what had appeared to them; that there was no credit to be given to the two witnesses on the side of the prosecution, and therefore found the prisoner

NOT GUILTY.

It still remains for us to make a few observations on the above extraordinary trial. Nothing that may now be said can in any manner affect Captain Kimber; as he has been acquitted, and cannot be tried a second time for the same offence.

We shall not declare what impressions we lie under as to the guilt or innocence of Capt. Kimber; but lay before the public a few points, from which they may draw such conclusions as their feelings and reason shall dictate.

And first we shall ask, why was there not such a defence set up by Captain Kimber, as could, in the minds of the people, have acquitted him of the horrid act which was sworn against him? Did he bring forward a single witness to contradict the charges of his accusers? What became of all the seamen and servants on board his ship, who were in England at the time he was apprehended, and who might have been brought into Court to declare at once that the prisoner did not commit murder; without having recourse to the miserable shift of proving perjury against Mr. Dowling and Devereux, in points that had nothing to do with the prosecution? Were none of the RECOVERY'S crew to be found, or was Captain Kimber afraid that they would have all conspired against his life?

One of the witnesses on the side of the prosecution said, that all the crew were taken up at Bristol, and sent out of the way. The event has given us no reason to doubt the truth of this assertion.

As to Mr. Dowling's not having disclosed the murder when he came on shore, nor keeping a complete journal, these are circumstances which those persons who know any thing of ships in general or the African slave trade, will pay no attention to. Journals, which are considered mere matters of form, are generally imperfect, and the barbarous treatment of slaves on board the ships is so frequent, as to be looked upon with indifference. Perhaps Mr. Dowling, perhaps the whole crew might have conceived that the killing of a slave on board a ship was an offence not punishable by law.

As there was no other evidence to support the second indictment, than what supported the first, the Jury also acquitted the prisoner on it.

The trial lasted near five hours. His Royal Highness the Duke of Clarence was present the whole time, and appeared from his looks and gestures, to be particularly interested, in favour of the man who was accused of having murdered a slave.

FINIS.

9 789362 096760